PETER RABBIT'S 75th BIRTHDAY
EXHIBITION

PETER RABBIT'S
75th BIRTHDAY EXHIBITION

A SOUVENIR CATALOGUE

THE NATIONAL BOOK LEAGUE
7 Albemarle Street London W1

Catalogue of the exhibition held at the National Book League
16th December 1976–14th January 1977.

ISBN 85353 254 0
Printed in Great Britain by Henry Stone & Son (Printers) Ltd., Banbury

Acknowledgements

During a period of over 20 years, the foresight and generosity of Mr Leslie Linder, ably assisted by his sister Miss Enid Linder, enabled him to collect from all over the world original pictures, manuscripts and letters relating to Beatrix Potter with the purpose of securing them for the nation. A charitable Trust was set up in 1970 and a considerable selection of Beatrix Potter's work became the Leslie Linder Collection housed at the National Book League. After Mr Linder's death a further collection went to the Victoria and Albert Museum as the Leslie Linder Bequest. From these two collections it has been possible to form a very substantial basis for Peter Rabbit's 75th Birthday Exhibition.

Our thanks are due to Mrs Anne Clarke, Librarian of the National Book League and Miss Irene Whalley of the Victoria and Albert Museum for selecting the exhibits on view, also to Mr Christopher Hanson-Smith of the National Trust, Ambleside, for the loan of Book Pictures and items relating to Beatrix Potter's schoolroom, and to Frederick Warne & Co. Ltd.

The exhibition in the N.B.L. Gallery was conceived and designed by Bryan Forbes, Ken Bridgeman and Ray Simm.

We would like to express our thanks to Edmond Chilton of the Rank Organisation for providing the replica setting to Miss Potter's schoolroom, which was made by the craftsmen of Pinewood Studios. Equally, our thanks go to Nat Cohen of EMI Film Distributors for allowing us to screen selections from the film *The Tales of Beatrix Potter*.

This catalogue was prepared by Keith Clark.

BEATRIX POTTER 1866–1943

BEATRIX POTTER was born in London on July 28th, 1866, and lived at Number Two, Bolton Gardens, Kensington. Both her parents were well off, having inherited their money from the Lancashire textile industry. Her grandfather, Edmund Potter who married Jessie Crompton, was head of one of the largest calico printing works in Europe and lived at Camfield Place, Hertfordshire, a stately country house with its fine trees, its lake and 300 acres of pasture land.

Her father, Rupert Potter, lived in retirement. He belonged to several London clubs, and numbered amongst his friends such distinguished people as Sir John Millais, the painter, and John Bright, the statesman. Mr Gaskell, husband of the well-known novelist, was also a great friend.

As a child, Beatrix Potter often stayed at Camfield Place, and was devoted to her grandmother. In her mid-twenties she referred to it as 'the place I love best in the world. . . . I remember when I was a child lying in a crib in the nursery bedroom under the tyranny of a cross old nurse—I used to be awakened at four in the morning by the song of the birds in the elm. I can feel the diamond-pattern of that old yellow crib printed against my cheek, as I lay with my head where my heels should be, staring backwards over my eyebrows at the plaster heads on the chimney piece, and a large watercolour alpine scene which I regarded with respectful awe.'

The Potters spent most of the year in London, but during the summer months they moved with their servants to furnished houses in Scotland or the Lake District. For twelve consecutive years Mr Potter rented Dalguise House, a seat on the banks of the Tay in the midst of lovely scenery, and it was here, from the age of five, that some of Beatrix Potter's happiest childhood days were spent.

It was after their first summer at Dalguise that Beatrix Potter's brother Bertram was born, and as he grew older, the children had much in common; they shared a love of nature, kept numerous pets, and were keenly interested in drawing and painting. Not only did they have wonderful opportunities for studying nature during these Scottish holidays, but they also enjoyed the company of her father's distinguished friends who were invited there for the fishing and shooting. Mr Bright would often take the children for walks on Sunday afternoons—fishing was not allowed on Sundays.

Of Mr Gaskell she wrote some charming recollections. 'Oh how plainly I see it again. He is sitting comfortably in the warm sunshine on the doorstep at Dalguise, in his grey coat and old felt hat. The newspaper lies on his knees, suddenly he looks up with his gentle smile. There are sounds of pounding footsteps. The blue-bottles whizz off the path. A little girl in a print frock and striped stockings bounds to his side and offers him a bunch of meadowsweet. He just says "thank-you-dear" and puts his arm round her. The bees hum round the flowers, the air is laden with the smell of roses, Sandy lies in his accustomed place against the doorstep.'

Easter holidays were usually spent in the West Country, and many of Beatrix Potter's sketches at places such as Falmouth and Sidmouth were later used as backgrounds for her illustrations for *The Tale of Little Pig Robinson*, one of the earliest stories to be written and the last to be published.

It was Miss Hammond, her governess, who realized that Beatrix Potter had an exceptional gift for drawing and painting, and encouraged and helped her in every way she could. The earliest drawings that have survived, of which the date is known, go back to the summer of 1875 when Beatrix Potter was nearly nine years old. As the years passed by she devoted an increasing amount of time to drawing and painting until her work included Interiors, Landscapes, Village Scenes, Gardens and Flowers, Still Life, Natural History and Animal Studies.

Once when referring to her work, she wrote: 'It is all the same, drawing, painting, modelling, the irresistible desire to copy any beautiful object which strikes the eye. Why cannot one be content to look at it? I cannot rest, I must draw, however poor the result.' Sir John Millais also encouraged her in her work; he once said to her, 'Plenty of people can *draw*, but *you* have observation.'

It is interesting to learn that in her fifteenth year Beatrix Potter attended a course of drawing lessons at the Science and Art Department of the Committee of Council on Education, where she received an Art Student's Certificate of Second Grade for Freehand Drawing, Practical Geometry, Linear Perspective and Model Drawing. At seventeen, Beatrix Potter attended classes on oil painting. In referring to these classes she wrote: 'Have begun a head of myself which promises surprisingly well—I am using my old paints and medium, and Rowney's rough canvas (I have the double primed)'—but her work in this medium does not appear to have survived.

When about fourteen years of age, Beatrix Potter invented a code-alphabet, which until she was thirty, she used for keeping a journal. In this journal she wrote accounts of the people she met, of the current affairs of the day, and of her many and varied interests. While there are gaps in the sequence of events, there are also long periods of day to day entries. Towards the end of her life Beatrix Potter wrote: 'When I was young I already had the itch to write without having any material to write about'. When the idea of a journal came to her, she found plenty of material to write about, and in a quiet and unobtrusive manner developed her powers of writing. As she left no key to the code, it is concluded that the journal was written entirely for her own use.

For several years from the age of sixteen, Beatrix Potter made a point of visiting the important exhibitions at the Royal Academy and at other art galleries, where she studied the pictures critically and reviewed those which appealed to her most.

Beatrix Potter also had many other interests—history, politics, literature, geology, natural history, botany, and for a period of about ten years she made an intensive study of fungi, collecting and painting every variety she could find. This collection of water-colours was eventually left to the Armitt Library at Ambleside, Westmorland, where it may be seen today. The specimens came largely from Scotland and the Lake District.

In 1896 Beatrix Potter was working on the preparation of a paper 'On the Germination of the Spores of *Agaricineae*', developing her own theories, which were well in advance of her time. The paper was read at a Meeting of the Linnean Society of London on April 1st 1897.

From time to time Beatrix Potter had sold an occasional drawing, but it was not until 1890 that any of her work was actually published. An idea to sell a set of designs to the trade arose from the success of some Christmas Cards 'which were put under the plates at breakfast and proved a five minutes wonder. I referred to them the other day and found my uncle had forgotten their existence, but he added with laughable inconsistency that any publisher would snap at them'. So Beatrix Potter prepared a set of six designs and offered them to Marcus Ward for the sum of £6. Marcus Ward was chosen first, because she had toned the colours from one of their Almanacs—they came back by return of post. The next firm she approached was Hildesheimer & Faulkner, who immediately recognized the merit of her designs and sent a cheque for £6. In due course these and other designs were published as Christmas and New Year cards, each card bearing the initials H.B.P. (Helen Beatrix Potter). They were also used to illustrate someone else's rhymes in a little booklet called *A Happy Pair*, which was sold at 4½ d.

Beatrix Potter related how on the excitement of receiving the cheque—'My first act was to give Bounce (what an investment that rabbit has been in spite of the hutches) a cupful of hemp seeds, the consequence being that when I wanted to draw him next morning he was partially intoxicated and wholly unmanageable. Then I retired to bed, and lay awake chuckling till two in the morning, and afterwards had the impression that Bunny came to my bedside in a white cotton night cap and tickled me with his whiskers.'

[The story of how Beatrix Potter's Tale of Peter Rabbit *came to be written and illustrated, privately printed in 1901 and finally published by Frederick Warne in 1902 is told in detail on pages 11–14.]*

In 1903 *The Tale of Squirrel Nutkin* and *The Tailor of Gloucester* were printed by Frederick Warne, in the latter case with some of the rhymes omitted, as anticipated by Beatrix Potter. From now onwards, year by year, fresh titles were added to the series, all of which were planned in close co-operation with the firm of Frederick Warne, and led to Beatrix Potter's friendship with Norman Warne, the youngest member of the publishing house. In the summer of 1905 they became engaged, but a few months later, when the planning of an *Appley Dapply* book of rhymes was practically finished, Norman Warne died suddenly, and the book was never completed.

After Norman Warne died, Beatrix Potter bought Hill Top Farm at Sawrey, Westmorland, and her interests now became centred on her new home in the Lake District. She built an extension to the farmhouse, reserving the main part for her own use, intending to pay occasional visits. It was not long, however, before she was spending all her spare time there.

Beatrix Potter's work now took on fresh colour from her surroundings. The buttercup meadow across the road, the winding lane up the hillside, the cottage doorways and their colourful gardens—all were used as background material for her stories. The interior of the quaint old farmhouse was depicted in *The Roly-Poly Pudding*; the beautiful garden at Hill Top in *The Tale of Tom Kitten*; the farmland in *The Tale of Jemima Puddle-Duck*; while Sawrey village was used for backgrounds for *The Pie and the Patty-Pan* and *Ginger and Pickles*; and the countryside around Sawrey for *The Tale of Mr Tod* and *Pigling Bland*.

In October 1913, Beatrix Potter married Mr William Heelis, a solicitor who had acted for her when buying property in the Lake District. After her marriage she felt that Hill Top was too small and moved to Castle Cottage, a converted farmhouse close by. From the bottom of their garden at Castle Cottage, they could look across the meadows and see Hill Top Farm.

Beatrix Potter, the writer, now became Mrs Heelis, the sheep farmer. The majority of her time was spent in managing her farms and in rearing her flocks of Herdwick sheep of which she was very proud.

During the years which followed, Beatrix Potter gradually bought land with a view to the preservation of the Lake District for the Nation. Eventually she bequeathed to the National Trust about half the village of Sawrey as well as many other properties, amounting to several thousand acres.

Only a few more books were published after her marriage, and these were largely based on fragments of left-overs from earlier writings. Thus, the *Appley Dapply* and *Cecily Parsley* books of nursery rhymes were based on the contents of her 1905 *Appley Dapply*—the pictures being redrawn and a selection of the rhymes used. *The Fairy Caravan*, published in 1929, is of particular interest to the inhabitants of Sawrey and the Lake District, as it contains many references to her farm animals and drawings of the locality.

Although Beatrix Potter's new home was at Castle Cottage, Mrs Storey, who lived at Hill Top, and remembered her well, told how she loved her old home best, and how during the last few years of her life she would often come round to Hill Top, arranging and sorting her papers and her other treasured possessions. Mrs Storey said, 'She liked to come and go unnoticed, and to be left quite alone with her memories of the past; and I would never come into that part of the house when Mrs Heelis was there, although on cold, dark, winter afternoons I often wished I could bring in cups of hot tea or cocoa to warm her.'

Beatrix Potter was evidently thinking of the years to come when people might want to know more about her and about the Hill Top she loved. She was preparing the way by writing little notes containing information, which were slipped in amongst her papers, attached to the backs of pictures hanging on the walls, and placed on other items of special interest. Similarly, at Castle Cottage, she had already sorted through her many drawings in their colourful hand-made portfolios, adding here and there titles, dates, and sundry remarks.

It was probably the effect of these cold, late, winter afternoons spent at Hill Top which hastened the attack of bronchitis from which Beatrix Potter died on the 22nd of December 1943, at the age of seventy-seven; but her work lives on and is a source of delight to young and old, not only in this country but throughout many parts of the world.   L. LINDER

10

INTRODUCING PETER RABBIT

The story of *The Tale of Peter Rabbit,* published seventy-five years ago this year, actually begins in the 1890s, when Beatrix Potter, then in her mid-twenties, purchased a young rabbit in the Uxbridge Road, a main thoroughfare in London's Shepherds Bush area. Beatrix Potter paid only four shillings and sixpence for him, a modest sum when one considers that Peter Rabbit was to become perhaps the most well-known animal in children's literature.

The story of Peter Rabbit and his mis-adventures in Mr McGregor's garden began as a letter to a sick child, Noel Moore. Noel was the eldest of seven children born to Annie Moore, who, as Annie Carter, had come to know Beatrix by being employed as her companion and tutor in German. The twenty-year-old Annie and the seventeen-year-old pupil became close friends, a relationship which survived even after Annie Carter had resigned her position in the Potter household after a year or two in order to get married. Beatrix Potter often visited Annie Moore and her husband at their Wandsworth home, and was a great favourite with their children.

When Noel Moore became ill in 1893, Beatrix Potter was away from the capital, spending the summer with her parents at Eastwood, a house on the Atholl Estate beside the river Tay in Perthshire. As she was unable to visit the sick boy, she sent him an eight-page letter, illustrated with sixteen really delightful pencil sketches, which began:

My dear Noel
    I don't know what to write to you, so I shall tell you a story about four little rabbits whose names were—Flopsy, Mopsy, Cottontail and Peter. They lived with their mother in a sand bank under the root of a big fir tree.

The story-letter, comprising basically the same story which was later to become so familiar with millions of children all over the world, was the first of many delightfully illustrated stories she wrote as letters to the Moore children and others concerning the actual and imaginary antics of her pets.

A few years after sending the Peter Rabbit letter, Beatrix Potter considered making the story into a book and borrowed the letter from Mrs Moore, who had kept all the letters neatly tied in ribbon, in order to make copies. The text she wrote into a stiff-covered exercise book, whilst she prepared the forty-two pen and ink sketches on separate paper which were tucked by their corners into corner slots cut in the pages of the book. The frontispiece, of Mrs Rabbit giving a dose of camomile tea to Peter who is suffering in bed from over-eating, was coloured by hand. The exercise book was labelled with the rather cumbersome title: "The Tale of Peter Rabbit and Mr McGregor's Garden, by H.B. Potter." It is interesting to note the use of the full initials, for she was actually christened Helen Beatrix and signed most of her early works with both initials even though she was always known to family and friends as Beatrix.

One of the people to whom the manuscript was shown was Canon H.D. Rawnsley, a founder member of the National Trust who had come to know the Potter family on their numerous summer holidays spent in his beloved Lake District. The warm, friendly manner of the clergyman, and the similarities of interests and hobbies, notably art and photography, led to Rawnsley becoming a close friend of Rupert Potter and of his daughter. Rawnsley, himself the author of a number of books, saw the potential in Beatrix Potter's proposed book and offered to aid her in getting it published by submitting the manuscript to publishers on her behalf. During 1900, *The Tale of Peter Rabbit* was submitted to at least six major publishers, all of whom rejected it and by 1901 Beatrix Potter had decided to pay for the book to be privately printed. On July 23rd, she commissioned two hundred and fifty copies to be printed by the London firm of Strangeways and Sons—whose offices were in Tower Street, Cambridge Circus—printers recommended by her friend, Miss Woodward, of the Natural History Museum.

The book, a neat looking publication bound in green paper cut flush to the pages, was ready on December 16, 1901. Forty-two black and white illustrations were reproduced from zinc blocks made by Art Reproductions of Fetter Lane, London, and the colour frontispiece was produced (by the three-colour process) by Hentschel of Fleet Street. It was sold to relatives and friends at one shilling and two pence each and within a couple of weeks had proved so popular that a second edition of two hundred copies was commissioned from Strangeways. A few minor alterations were made in text and punctuation, a stiff olive-green cover with rounded spine was used instead of the lighter green paper cover of the first edition, and the date "Feb. 1902" was incorporated into the title-page.

During the production of the privately printed editions, Rawnsley had not lost his confidence in the book and in 1901 he wrote to Frederick Warne and Sons, one of the publishers who had originally rejected the manuscript, offering them his own version of the story written in verse to be illustrated by Beatrix Potter's drawings. The good clergyman's version, complete with worthy morals, began:

There were four little bunnies
—no bunnies were sweeter
Mopsy and Cotton-tail
Flopsy and Peter

> They lived in a sand-bank
> as here you may see
> At the foot of a fir
> —a magnificent tree.

Thankfully, Warne replied to Rawnsley on September 18, 1901, that they preferred the more straightforward text by Beatrix Potter. Before the privately printed edition had been delivered to Beatrix Potter, Warne had reconsidered their decision and had decided to accept *Peter Rabbit*—if Beatrix Potter was willing to prepare colour illustrations instead of black-and-white, and if satisfactory arrangements with regard to royalties could be made.

Warne restricted her to thirty pictures and a frontispiece, and so eleven of her line illustrations were not redrawn for the Warne edition and the corresponding text transferred to other pages. In three cases, the text was deleted altogether, to be re-introduced two years later in *The Tale of Benjamin Bunny*. The redrawing of the illustrations seems to have caused some problems, as is clearly shown in the correspondence between author and publisher reprinted in Leslie Linder's superbly authoritative *History of the Writings of Beatrix Potter* (F. Warne, 1971). Whilst being extremely imaginative as a writer, Beatrix Potter appears to have lacked imagination to the same level when it came to illustrating, indeed she is reported to have said to the Westmorland artist, Delmar Banner: "I can't invent, I only copy." There is perhaps some truth in this modest statement, for almost all the backgrounds to her illustrations were based on actual places. The vegetable garden, fir tree and wicker gate which feature in *Peter Rabbit* were based on places around Keswick and, of course, Hill Top Farm and the village of Sawrey are easily recognised in the illustrations to many of her later stories. The accuracy with which she "copied" the backgrounds, however, can be a little disconcerting for the visitor to the Lake District village in which she later made her home as her settings are so familiar that one almost expects to see her characters walking through the streets and lanes of Sawrey.

In the same way, she used her pets—and those of her friends and neighbours—as models for the animals in her illustrations. This proved awkward in the preparation of *Peter Rabbit*, for the pet died before Beatrix Potter began the drawings for the Warne edition. She wrote in a copy of the privately printed edition of *The Tale:*

> In affectionate remembrance of poor old Peter Rabbit, who died on the 26th of January 1901 at the end of his ninth year ... whatever the limitations of his intellect or outward shortcomings of his fur, and his ears and toes, his disposition was uniformly amiable and his temper unfailingly sweet. An affectionate companion and a quiet friend.

The two human characters in the original *Peter Rabbit*, Mr and Mrs McGregor, also caused some problems in completing the illustrations and in the end the picture of Mrs McGregor and the pie was not used as Warnes were not happy about the "old woman's face". Beatrix Potter was not as competent an artist of the human form as she was of animals or landscapes, perhaps because she did not have models to base them on. She has stated that Mr McGregor was not based on any one person, but she did once suggest that Mrs McGregor was a caricature of herself. If this is so, the caricature was a very unflattering one indeed!

Beatrix Potter's own feelings about the drawings for *Peter Rabbit* were revealed in a letter she wrote to her publisher on May 8, 1902, which illustrates something of the modesty of the artist as well as a certain lack of confidence in her own work:

> I wish the drawings had been better; I dare say they
> may look better when reduced; but I am becoming so
> tired of them. I begin to think they are positively bad ...

Frederick Warne produced a first edition of six thousand copies in 1902. It was printed by Edmund Evans (The Racquet Court Press), an engraver and printer who had, in the latter decades of the previous century, been instrumental in bringing to the public's attention the work of such much-loved artist/writers as Caldecott, Crane and Greenaway. The colour illustrations, like the colour frontispiece in the privately printed editions, were made by Hentschel and the book was issued in two bindings: an ordinary binding which sold for one shilling and a cloth-bound version which retailed at one shilling and sixpence. Both versions had a coloured illustration pasted down on to the front cover.

During the first year of publication, *The Tale of Peter Rabbit* sold over 20,000 copies, and during the past twenty-five years the sale figures have reached an astonishingly high figure. Its success has not only been in the English-speaking countries, for *Peter Rabbit* has been translated into German, French, Welsh, Italian, Swedish, Japanese, Spanish and a host of other languages, including Latin! There can be no doubt that *Peter Rabbit* is Beatrix Potter's best-loved and best-known book, although she stated on many occasions that her favourite of all books was *The Tailor of Gloucester*. In 1940 Beatrix Potter wrote in a letter to a friend in America: "I have never quite understood the secret of Peter's perennial charm. Perhaps it is because he and his little friends keep on their way; busily absorbed in their own doings".

KEITH CLARK

THE NATIONAL BOOK LEAGUE GALLERY

The exhibition, designed by Bryan Forbes, Ken Bridgeman and Ray Simm, shows the origin of Beatrix Potter's first book, *Peter Rabbit*, and how some of her subsequent stories for children came to be written and illustrated.

THE BIRTH OF PETER RABBIT

This first section covers the origins of the story of Peter Rabbit. Here we see the story letter she wrote to Noel Moore in September 1893 in which Peter Rabbit's escapades in Mr McGregor's garden are set out for the first time. One can well imagine the delight with which this must have been received by the sick five-year-old child. It is also easy to see why, when Beatrix Potter asked to borrow back the letter some years later to make it into a book, she found that this and subsequent story letters to the Moore children had been stored away so carefully. The story was fictitious, of course, but Peter was a real rabbit and one of the many pets which inhabited Beatrix Potter's world. These animals often provided "sitters" for watercolours—like the delightful one shown here of Peter lying on a rug in the schoolroom at Bolton Gardens—as well as forming the characters of her story letters and later her popular books.

THE PLANNING OF THE TALE

Having decided to turn the story letter into a book, Beatrix Potter began to lengthen and rewrite Peter's adventures and work on the illustrations. Much of this planning was done at Tenby, where the Potters were spending the summer of 1900. However, we can see from the watercolours she made of Tenby scenes that not all of her holiday was spent working on the proposed book.

The manuscript book of *Peter Rabbit* was sent to at least six publishers, all of whom rejected it. One of these was Frederick Warne and Co., who gave the story's publication serious consideration, as is shown in their letter to Beatrix Potter rejecting the book.

Even though she had been unsuccessful in persuading a publisher to take on the story, she still felt that it would make a nice book, and so commissioned a London printing firm to produce 250 copies of it. These books, bound in grey-green paper boards, were ready on December 16, 1901. This date is important, for December 16th is also the date on the letter from Warne to Beatrix Potter informing her that they had reconsidered their decision.

THE PRIVATE EDITION

One can see from these reproductions of pages from the privately printed edition of *The Tale of Peter Rabbit* that the published story is similar to that in the story letter to Noel Moore and that the positioning of text and illustrations follow the pattern to become standard in most of the subsequent books. The size of the book is interesting, for this was followed almost exactly by Warne and complied with her belief that small children preferred small books which fitted easily into their small hands.

The major difference between the private and the Warne edition is obvious for, with the exception of the frontispiece, all the private edition illustrations were pen sketches reproduced in monochrome.

There were also many more illustrations in the private edition for some had to be omitted from the Warne edition, like this really delightful one of Peter Rabbit hiding beneath a bush.

THE FIRST EDITION

As is shown by the correspondence between Beatrix Potter and her publisher, reprinted in Leslie Linder's authoritative *History of the Writings of Beatrix Potter*, she took a great interest in every aspect of her first book's production. She took a special interest in the reproduction of her drawings, as can be seen in the two letters exhibited here, one of which goes into great detail as to the economics of block making, the other containing various enquiries about the reproduction of her work. The latter, dated January 19th, 1902, contains an interesting postscript informing Warne that no less a critic than Sherlock Holmes' creator had commented on the private edition of *Peter Rabbit*: "I do not know if it is worth mentioning—But Dr Conan Doyle had a copy for his children and he has a good opinion of the story and words".

The preparation of the text for the book did not cause too many diffi-culties, for it is very similar to the second printing of the private edition, which was produced only a few weeks after the first printing. The illustrations, however, took more preparation. Always a perfectionist, Beatrix Potter offered Warne alternatives to certain illustrations for them to choose the one most suitable for reproduction. In some cases, such as the three drawings she submitted for the title-page illustration of Peter Rabbit, these alternatives show only very slight variation.

PETER RABBIT

Original manuscript and illustrations

In this section of the exhibition we can see the delicate detailed original watercolours used in the first Warne edition of *Peter Rabbit*. It will be noticed that there are not as many illustrations in the Warne edition as in the original, for Frederick Warne restricted her to thirty text illustrations whereas she had used forty-two in the private edition. Selecting the illustrations to appear in the book must have been a difficult task for Beatrix Potter. A charming watercolour illustration of a robin perched on a shoe illustrating the line "And the other shoe amongst the potatoes", was not used. Some of the original drawings which were selected for reproduction in the first Warne edition were taken out in subsequent editions, especially after the fourth printing. For instance, the drawing of fir trees exhibited here was used as a background for the picture of "Peter never stopped running or looked behind him till he got home to the big fir tree", an illustration which appeared in the first Warne edition but was dropped after the fourth printing.

The drawing of Mrs McGregor serving the pie to her husband was also dropped after the fourth printing, after an interesting but chequered history. The black-and-white illustration of this scene in the private edition was rather poor, and the first drawing she submitted to Warne was not that much more successful. Eventually she redrew Mrs McGregor as a much younger woman—she once wrote that it was a caricature of herself—which was accepted by the publisher only to be taken out with three others after the fourth printing so that the uniform endpapers could be incorporated for the first time in this *Tale*.

Mr McGregor's picture in *Peter Rabbit* was equally unsuccessful, and in the letter to Warne dated May 2nd, 1902, we can read a rather pithy comment: "My brother is sarcastic about the figures, what you and he take for Mr McGregor's nose was intended for his ear, not his nose at all".

Another problem she had to deal with was not caused by the illustrations but by her father, as we can read in her letter of May 22nd in which she warns her publisher that Rupert Potter might visit them to look over their agreement: "I think it better to mention beforehand that he is sometimes a little difficult".

Throughout the summer of 1902, Beatrix Potter was correcting proofs of the text and illustrations with her usual meticulous care. In a letter sent with the corrected proofs, dated August 17th, she makes a modest comment which shows that she had no inkling of the success that the *Tale of Peter Rabbit* was to become: "I hope the little book will be a success, there seems to be a great deal of trouble being taken with it".

BEATRIX POTTER'S WORLD

This display attempts to give an impression of Beatrix Potter's world through some of the items with which she surrounded herself—both at Bolton Gardens and later at Hill Top.

The setting is based on her schoolroom at number 2 Bolton Gardens, South Kensington, as seen in a pen-and-ink drawing she made in 1885. Some of the items, like the fender in the foreground of this pen drawing, were later taken to Hill Top when she moved to Sawrey. The rug which lay on the floor in front of the fire was the one on which Peter Rabbit lay for the watercolour exhibited in an earlier section. The paintings, set of illustrated plates, sketches and etchings by members of her family are interesting, for she was not the only Potter to have talent in this direction.

When one visits Hill Top one can never get away from the books, for the house was used in the illustrations to certain *Tales* and is full of items one associates with certain stories. For instance, the flat iron is like the one seen in *Mrs Tiggy-Winkle*. The "mouse box" was given by Beatrix Potter to her mother, Christmas 1899. The little mice are printed in watercolour, cut out, and pasted on. The box, which is made of beech wood, cost 6¾d. The miniature letters are delightful items, sent to her children friends as if from the animal characters, in some cases sent in little mailbags she had made.

Finally, the watercolour entitled "November Day", shows the scene from a window of the Potter home in Bolton Gardens, looking out over the gardens situated in this fashionable part of London.

With this very graphic view of Beatrix Potter's world, we leave Peter Rabbit for a while to take a look at some of the books which followed. As we shall see, the history of Peter Rabbit does not finish here, however, for Peter turns up in a number of the later books, especially *Benjamin Bunny*, sometimes named but more often just one of the characters in the illustrations. There was also the *Peter Rabbit Almanac* (1929) and a *Peter Rabbit Painting Book*.

JEMIMA PUDDLE-DUCK

Jemima Puddle-Duck is based in and around Hill Top, Beatrix Potter's farm in the Lake District village of Sawrey. So little has this area changed that one can easily recognize those scenes which were used as backgrounds for her illustrations in this story. Compare her illustration to page 44 of *Jemima Puddle-Duck*, in which the Tower Bank Arms (the village pub) forms the background, with a photograph of the actual scene from the same angle taken this year, and it can be clearly seen that Sawrey has not altered that much since the beginning of the century. The wrought-iron gate near the rhubarb patch in the illustration to page 12, is also still to be seen at Hill Top Farm, which itself has changed very little as we can see in the view of it in the last illustration (page 58) to the duck story.

One can hazard a guess from the *Jemima Puddle-Duck* illustrations that foxgloves must have been one of Beatrix Potter's favourite flowers, for they are included in no less than five of the book drawings. These colourful and stately flowers abound in Sawrey during the early summer months and Beatrix Potter painted a number of pleasing watercolours of them, the one exhibited here being interesting for it also bears another flower drawing (of canterbury bells) on the back.

Jemima was a real duck who lived at the farm, and at the end of the manuscript there is a photograph she took of the real Jemima.

The fields, meadows and woods of Hill Top also figure in the book's illustrations, especially that part of the farmland which has come to be known as "Jemima Puddle-Duck's Wood". This wood looks out over Esthwaite Water, a view totally unchanged since Beatrix Potter painted the watercolour of 1911 included in this section, the same view used as a background for the illustration on page 16 of the current edition of the *Tale*.

JEREMY FISHER

The Tale of Jeremy Fisher is an interesting book for, even before Warne published it in 1906, a skeleton of the story had originally appeared in a children's annual in the middle of the previous decade and it was Beatrix Potter's first substantial excursion into print.

Jeremy Fisher is also a character with a lot of charm and is very vividly portrayed in the illustrations, perhaps the reason why this animal character comes over so well in the superb ballet film of *The Tales of Beatrix Potter.* Indeed, Jeremy Fisher might well have been illustrated with a ballet in mind, for we can see in many of the illustrations, like that of the frog seated, reading on a window sill (page 8) that she drew Jeremy Fisher wearing dainty slippers very similar to ballet shoes and she often depicted him in ballet-like positions. As we shall see later in a section devoted to the ballet film, the designers of the film costumes and sets faithfully reproduced the original drawings. This can be shown by comparing stills from the film with some of her original illustrations, like that of Jeremy Fisher sitting on a waterlily leaf fishing—a number of sketches for which are exhibited in this section as well as a pen and watercolour.

The Tale of Jeremy Fisher, like so many of the books, originated in a story letter. It was then set on the River Tay, where the Potters were spending the summer of 1893, but the backgrounds to the actual book illustrations, like the watercolour of waterlily leaves shown here, were actually drawn at Esthwaite Water.

SQUIRREL NUTKIN

Squirrel Nutkin, published in 1903, was the second book by Beatrix Potter to have been published by Warne, although *The Tailor of Gloucester* had appeared earlier privately printed in the same manner as *Peter Rabbit. Nutkin* is set in the wooded grounds and surrounding countryside of Lingholm and Fawe Park, two large houses, set on the edge of Derwentwater, where the Potters spent summer holidays. Owl Island is in reality St. Herbert's Island, opposite Lingholm, and we know from the inscription on the back of a photograph of a fine old oak tree that "Old Brown's Oak", a detailed study of which is exhibited, was actually in the grounds of Lingholm. The story is about red squirrels, sadly so rare in so many parts of the country but still to be seen in large numbers in these woods, which must have been even more prolific in her day. Her sketchbooks for the summer of 1901 are full of sketches of red squirrels drawn at Derwentwater, but the model for the final illustrations was a squirrel she bought sometime between November and December 1902 and drew at home.

Old Brown, the owl, was drawn at the Zoological Gardens in London. We know that she took considerable trouble getting him right, even getting her brother to help improve one of the drawings.

As can be seen from the original drawing, the title-page illustration to

Squirrel Nutkin is rather out of character, being much blacker than is typical.

Most of the Beatrix Potter books were issued in two separate editions—in a normal binding and a deluxe binding. The deluxe edition of *Squirrel Nutkin* was bound in a floral fabric (she wrote of it as a "flowered lavender chintz") manufactured by her grandfather's firm, Edmund Potter & Co of Dinting Vale, Manchester—one of the largest calico printers in Europe. Warne originally approached her with the suggestion that a brocade should be used on the deluxe edition, and, as we can read in her reply, dated March 12, 1903, she agreed that a pretty cloth binding would induce more people to buy the slightly more expensive edition. It was also in this letter that she suggests using a fabric manufactured by her grandfather's firm.

PIGLING BLAND

The Tale of Pigling Bland, first published in 1913, is the story of two of the pigs at Hill Top Farm, Alexander and Pigling Bland. The illustrations were set in and around Hill Top; for instance the crossroads behind the farm on the road to Lakeside and Hawkshead is featured in the frontispiece drawing. It is to be seen today exactly as painted, and is so faithfully reproduced on the frontispiece that, if you stand at the crossroads, you can almost imagine the two pigs walking down the road towards Sawrey in front of you.

The exhibited frontispiece watercolour was not the one used in the book, however, for instead of both being dressed in green coats, one of the coats in the book drawing is brown. Beatrix Potter made an interesting note (presumably at a much later date) on the back of the duplicate: "This is much better than the one in the book". The farmyard scenes, such as the illustrations of Aunt Pettitoes feeding her piglets, were set at Hill Top Farm, but other local places were also used, including the kitchen of Spout House in Far Sawrey.

We can see in this section an unusual edition of *Pigling Bland*, for in 1921 it was produced in Braille by the Royal Institute for the Blind. Having her books issued so that blind children could also enjoy them greatly pleased Beatrix Potter, especially as many years earlier her mother had been one of those who gave up a great deal of time to transcribing books (by hand) for the Blind Association.

BENJAMIN BUNNY

The Tale of Benjamin Bunny, published in 1904, is a sequel to the adventures of Peter Rabbit in Mr McGregor's garden and relates how Benjamin and his cousin Peter return to the garden to retrieve the latter's lost clothes.

The backgrounds were drawn in the gardens of Fawe Park, near Keswick, where the Potters stayed in 1903. These gardens provided a wealth of scenes for her to paint and just before returning to London she wrote to Warne that she thought she had done about seventy backgrounds at Fawe Park, as well as miscellaneous sketches. Some of these backgrounds, such as the "walk on planks", the watercolour of lettuces, broad beans and others are to be seen in this section.

The frontispiece in *The Tale of Benjamin Bunny*, showing Mrs Rabbit in her shop, appeared in a different form as a black and white illustration in the privately printed edition of *Peter Rabbit*. The illustration originally intended for the frontispiece to *Benjamin Bunny* (of rabbits and flowers) was not used, but we can see from the intended frontispiece and the background picture that the drawing was put to good use, with the background being incorporated into the picture (page 39) of Peter letting go of the onions for the second time.

Like Peter Rabbit, Benjamin Bunny was in reality the name of one of Beatrix Potter's pets, known affectionately by her as "Bounce".

TALES OF BEATRIX POTTER

These sections are concerned with the ballet film 'Tales of Beatrix Potter' which was such a phenomenal success when it was presented by EMI Film Productions Ltd in 1971, and which continues to fill cinemas every time it is reissued.

The idea of adapting five of Beatrix Potter's *Tales, Jemima Puddle-Duck, Pigling Bland, Jeremy Fisher, Two Bad Mice* and *Squirrel Nutkin,* and including characters from her other books, not forgetting Peter Rabbit of course, came from Christine Edzard, who designed the sets and costumes, and her husband Richard Goodwin, who together with John Brabourne produced the film. Sir Frederick Ashton was the choreographer—and also danced Mrs Tiggy-Winkle—while other prominent members of the Royal Ballet danced the following characters:

Peter Rabbit	Alexander Grant	*Owl*	Leslie Edwards
Mrs. Tittlemouse	Julie Wood	*Tabitha Twitchit*	Sally Ashby
Johnny Town-Mouse	Keith Martin	*Town Mice, Pigs,*	
Jemima Puddle-Duck	Ann Howard	*Squirrels,*	
Fox	Robert Mead	*Country Mice*	Carole Ainsworth
Pigling Bland	Alexander Grant		Avril Bergen
Alexander	Garry Grant		Jill Cooke
Mrs. Pettitoes	Sally Ashby		Graham Fletcher
Pig-Wig	Brenda Last		Bridget Goodricke
Jeremy Fisher	Michael Coleman		Garry Grant
Tom Thumb	Wayne Sleep		Suzanna Raymond
Hunca Munca	Lesley Collier		Rosemary Taylor
Squirrel Nutkin	Wayne Sleep		Anita Young

Twelve-year-old Erin Geraghty played the young Beatrix Potter, Joan Benham the nurse and Wilfred Babbage the butler.

The Goodwins' house was turned into a workshop where the costumes were made and where much of the work on the wonderful masks took place. These masks were designed by Rostislav Doboujinsky, whose faithful copying of the book illustrations contributed so much to the film's success. John Lanchbery used Victorian and Edwardian tunes for music for the ballet and conducted the Orchestra of the Royal Opera House, Covent Garden. The Director was Reginald Mills and the Director of Photography was Austin Dempster. A book about how the film was made called *The Tale of the Tales* was written by Rumer Godden, who visited the sets and the Goodwin house to find the fascinating inside story.

A MICE MISCELLANY

Mice feature in a number of Beatrix Potter's books and make some of her best loved characters. Probably the best known of the mice stories are the misadventures of Tom Thumb and Hunca Munca, published as *The Tale of the Two Bad Mice* in 1904. These mice were based on two animals rescued from a mouse trap in the kitchen of Harescombe Grange, Gloucestershire.

Two illustrations from this book are featured in this section, one of a mouse and a cradle which is represented by two sketches and the title-page drawing. Also within this "mice miscellany" are various watercolours by Beatrix Potter featuring mice, one of the most delightful being the watercolour of a mouse reading a newspaper. This picture—note the creature's crossed feet—must certainly have been one of her favourites, for a black and white photograph of the painting was discovered amongst her papers at Hill Top. It is interesting to compare this original drawing, entitled "A Day's News", with the illustration used on the cover of *The Tailor of Gloucester*, for one was obviously the inspiration for the other.

The charming watercolour of a mouse knitting was used as an illustration to *Appley Dapply's Nursery Rhymes* (page 24)—a book she had originally planned as early as 1905. In fact as early as 1894, Beatrix Potter sold a picture of a mouse knitting to Ernest Nister for publication in one of their annuals.

The pictures sold to Nister (including a story later to become *Jeremy Fisher*) were not Beatrix Potter's only excursions into print in the 1890s, for she also sold a set of designs to Hildesheimer & Faulkner, some of which, like the design of a mouse in its nest, were published as Christmas and New Year cards.

The picture of the three mice seated at a table eating a Christmas meal, drawn in December 1893, was also presumably a Christmas card, but it is thought that this was drawn purely to be given to a relative or friend.

ENDPAPERS

The endpapers of the Beatrix Potter books, illustrated with small pictures of the animal characters, are a delightful and integral part of the Peter Rabbit books' charm.

The endpapers appeared for the first time in the first edition of *Squirrel Nutkin* in 1903. The design was slightly changed for *Benjamin Bunny* in 1904 and in each subsequent book the endpaper changes slightly as different characters are introduced. By observing the characters in these illustrated endpapers, it is possible to estimate when each book was published. For instance, Jeremy Fisher first makes an appearance in the endpapers of the book which followed it, *Tom Kitten* (1907), and that character is included for the first time in the following book, *Jemima Puddle-Duck* (1908), and so on.

Peter Rabbit and *Tailor of Gloucester* were first published with plain endpapers, but the illustrated endpapers were used from the 2nd printing of *The Tailor*, and from the 6th printing of *Peter Rabbit*.

Certain of the later books, including *Mr Tod, Pigling Bland* and the two nursery rhyme books, bore a different style of endpaper—a pictorial design containing a list of titles in the "Peter Rabbit Series" and most of the animal characters.

The endpaper for *Peter Rabbit's Almanac for 1929* was also different, containing small pictures of rabbits forming an upright rectangular frame for a drawing of a lettuce plant.

UNCLE REMUS

The six pencil drawings in this section illustrate the classic Uncle Remus story of Brer Rabbit and Brer Fox. They were made between 1893 and 1895 when Beatrix Potter was considering making the story into an illustrated book—one of a number of early ideas for books which never materialized.

Note the way she has put the lines of the text and a secondary picture around the main subject picture, utilizing almost every centimetre of the page. This is totally unlike her illustrations to the Peter Rabbit books, where a small illustration is set in a much larger page so that a lot of unused white space is around it, but it was a style that was quite fashionable amongst illustrators of the time.

TRANSLATIONS

Frederick Warne and Beatrix Potter first looked at the possibilities of translating some of the Peter Rabbit books into French and German as early as 1907. It appears that a French translation was made in that year, but Beatrix Potter did not like the way in which it had been translated.

In 1912 *Peter Rabbit* and *Jemima Puddle-Duck* were published in Dutch, and at the same time a Frenchwoman, Mlle. Victorine Ballon was working on the translation into French. The French edition of *Peter Rabit* ("Pierre Lapin") and *Benjamin Bunny* ("Jeannot Lapin") were not to see publication however until 1921.

Today, the Peter Rabbit books are known in translation all over the world, as can be seen in this display. Children in France, Germany, Holland, Italy, Spain, Sweden, Norway and Denmark can read some of the books in their own language, as indeed can the children in Japan. They have also been translated into Welsh and *Peter Rabbit* and *Jemima Puddle-Duck* have been translated into Latin.

Some of the titles have translated beautifully. In Sweden Squirrel Nutkin is known as "Kurre Nottpigg"; in Germany the Flopsy Bunnies are the "Hasenfamilie Plumps" and in Latin, Jemima has become "Jemima Anate-Aquatica". Surely the most amusing must be the German-Swiss translation of *Samuel Whiskers,* which becomes *Bernhard Schnauzbart*!

MISCELLANEOUS TALES

In an earlier section of this exhibition, we saw six drawings produced many years before *Peter Rabbit*, as illustrations for a proposed book of the Uncle Remus stories. This was only one of a number of ideas Beatrix Potter had for books, as we can see in some of the illustrations exhibited in this group.

Three watercolours illustrating Lewis Carroll's *Alice* are shown here, two of the white rabbit and one of two guinea-pigs, the white rabbit, a mouse and several other animals trying to revive the lizard Bill. The latter, dated "March 93" is not as graphic as the White Rabbit pictures, one of which shows the animal running forward, the other running away, and is not of the same quality as her later work and certainly not of the same imaginative quality as that of some of the illustrators who have illustrated the *Alice* books.

The sepia pen-and-ink drawing for the title-page or cover of *Puss-In-Boots* was drawn in May 1894 and, while this is quite successful, it is not as pleasing as the sepia drawing for the *Ali Baba and the Forty Thieves*, which is a fine illustration. The watercolour and a preliminary pen-and-ink of the two rabbits in the street were drawn in 1890 for a booklet, called *A Happy Pair*, published by Hildesheimer & Faulkner. This was one of a set of pictures used in the booklet, illustrating verse by Frederic Weatherly (better known as the pro-lific songwriter who composed "Roses of Picardy"). The drawing of the piebald guinea-pigs in a row running for their supper was one of a number of Christmas cards that Beatrix Potter drew for friends and relations, and guinea-pigs are shown gardening in a watercolour and preliminary sketch which are exhibited in this section of the exhibition. The "Guinea-pigs gardening" was painted in 1893, from animals loaned to her by a neighbour, and was later used (in *Appley Dapply*) to illustrate the lines: "We have a little garden, a garden of our own." "The rabbit's dream" is a particularly pleasing pen and ink study of a rabbit asleep in a bed surrounded by small drawings of rabbits from almost every con-ceivable angle. Interestingly the bed was the one in which Beatrix Potter slept when staying with her grandmother at Camfield Place.

Beatrix Potter, the illustrator of popular children's books, is only too well-known, but there are many aspects of Beatrix Potter the artist which are less well appreciated.

For instance, few of the many millions of parents who have read her books to their children perhaps have realized that Beatrix Potter was also a very talented watercolour landscape painter and much praised artist of scientific subjects.

This part of the exhibition in the Mark Longman Library is devoted to showing some of the facets of Beatrix Potter's art which are not directly related to her children's books.

SOURCES

After each of the following entries a reference number has been given to identify from which collection of Beatrix Potter's work that item has been loaned.

Those references preceded by the letters *BP* have been loaned from the Leslie Linder Bequest by the Victoria and Albert Museum.

Those preceded by *LLT* are from the Leslie Linder Trust collection housed in the Mark Longman Library of the National Book League.

CASE 1. BEATRIX POTTER'S EARLY WORK

These drawings and watercolours were made when Beatrix Potter was a young girl, the earliest having been drawn when she was only nine years old and already beginning to show that she was a potentially very talented artist.

The Pre-Raphaelite painter, Sir John Millais, once said to her that "Plenty of people can draw, but you and my son John have observation" and this is clearly to be seen in her early still life drawings which show an eye for detail and a confidence very unusual in one so young.

1 LEAF DESIGN
Crayon drawing, dated "14th. May 1879", 147 x 204mm. (on sheet 267 x 343mm.)
Linder suggests this drawing of a leaf was probably schoolwork done when she was twelve years old. (LLT: 1.B.4)

2 FRIEZE
Sepia watercolour with light pencil outlines, inscribed "June 82", 130 x 350mm.
A watercolour section of a frieze of flowers, berries and acanthus-like foliage. It is thought that this was probably schoolwork for Miss Cameron, who gave Beatrix Potter drawing lessons from 1878 to 1883. (BP 222)

3   GRAPES AND PEACHES
Watercolour, inscribed "July 1882", 231 x 267mm. (LLT: 1.A.4)

4   CARNATIONS
Watercolour, inscribed "September 2nd. 1880". 178 x 254mm.
Drawn when she was only 14 years old, probably schoolwork for her
governess Miss Hammond. (LLT: 10.A.3)

5   DORMOUSE
Transfer print, inscribed "H.B.P. 1880", 100 x 145mm.
When she was fourteen, Beatrix Potter experimented with a transfer
process and produced a number of prints of different animals, printed
in a violet ink. The transfer print exhibited is a delightful one, full of
life, illustrating a dormouse seated on a branch. (BP 558a)

6   FOXGLOVES AND PERIWINKLE
*Pencil drawing, inscribed "Helen Beatrix Potter Feb.9. 1876", 251 x
176mm.*
Drawn when she was only 9 years old, this pencil drawing shows an eye
for accurate draughtsmanship remarkable in one so young. Note the
full name signature, which is unusual on her drawings and only
appears on the very earliest works. (LLT: 10.A.1)

7   HIPS
Watercolour, 176 x 254mm.
Drawn when she was about twelve years old, this has been dated at a
later date by Beatrix Potter "1878 or 79". Extremely neat, showing
that, even at such an early age, Beatrix Potter was fully aware of how to
produce a three-dimensional effect. (LLT: 10.A.6)

8   HONEYSUCKLE
Watercolour, inscribed "June & July, 82", 176 x 252mm.
Drawn on a sheet of paper with large margins in which Beatrix Potter
has tried out some of her colours. (LLT: 10.A.4)

CASE 2 & 3.   INTERIORS

Beatrix Potter greatly loved to draw and paint interiors of fine
old houses full of beautiful furniture, and this section shows the insides
of many homes of her relatives, such as Gwaynynog in Denbigh and
Melford Hall in Suffolk.

Also exhibited are watercolours of houses in many parts of the
country which the Potter family rented for their long summer holidays,
like the lovely Lake District house, Lingholm, near Keswick.

One obvious characteristic of her work clearly shown in these
interiors is her well developed sense of perspective.

9 A WINTER EVENING

Watercolour, inscribed "A Winter Evening—H.B. Potter", 226 x 274mm.
Drawn in January 1900, showing the interior of Derwent Cottage, since renamed "Haskards"—a house in Winchelsea, Sussex, where the Potters spent the winter of 1899/1900. In a picture letter to Freda Moore from Derwent Cottage, Beatrix Potter wrote: "I am staying in such a funny old cottage . . . The ceiling of my bedroom is so low I can touch it with my hand, and there is a little lattice window just the right size for mice to peep out of". (LLT: 2.A.1)

10 DINING ROOM AT BEDFORD SQUARE

Watercolour, inscribed "8 Bedford Square. Nov. 1905. Beatrix Potter", 280 x 230mm. (effective size 200 x 195mm).
Interior of part of a room at number 8, Bedford Square, London, the home of the Warne family. Beatrix Potter was a regular visitor to her publisher's home and was, for a short time, engaged to be married to Norman Warne. This painting was executed soon after Norman Warne's sad death in 1905 and was given to Fruing Warne. (BP 284)

11 LIBRARY, WRAY CASTLE

Watercolour, inscribed on back "Wray Castle, July 1882", 350 x 250mm.
Between July 21st and October 31st, 1882, the Potters stayed in Wray Castle, an impressive Victorian castle built in 1845, not many miles from Sawrey. It was whilst here that the Potters became acquainted with Canon Rawnsley—a founder member of the National Trust, who later helped Beatrix Potter to find a publisher for *Peter Rabbit*. (BP 231)

12 SITTING ROOM, DERWENT COTTAGE

Pencil drawing, inscribed "Winchelsea, Feb 1st. 1900", on loose-leaf card, 139 x 227mm.
Illustrates the sitting room of Derwent Cottage, Winchelsea, Sussex. (LLT: 11.A.1.)

13 INTERIOR OF DRESSING ROOM

Pencil drawing, 200 x 252mm.
Believed to be of a room at Derwent Cottage, Winchelsea, Sussex, and to have been drawn in 1900. (LLT: 12.B.5)

14 INTERIOR OF A BARN

Grey brush work, inscribed "H.B.P. Sept. 91", 255 x 162mm.
Shows three farm cats in an old barn at Bedwell Lodge, Hertfordshire, where the Potters spent the summer of 1891. (LLT: 12.B.3)

15 FIREPLACE AT MELFORD HALL

Watercolour and pencil, inscribed "Christmas 03. Melford" and "H.B. Potter, Melford Hall, Suffolk", 227 x 189mm.

An unfinished watercolour of a tall, ornate fireplace with the pencil outline of a child seated in front of it. Melford Hall was the home of Sir William Hyde-Parker, who married Beatrix Potter's cousin, Ethel Leech, and the child outlined in the picture is Stephanie Hyde-Parker. On April 13th 1903, Beatrix Potter wrote from Melford to Norman Warne: "I have been able to draw an old fashioned fireplace here, very suitable for the tailor's kitchen; I will get on with the book as fast as I can" (the book in question being *Tailor of Gloucester*). Besides this watercolour, the Linder Trust collection also contains a watercolour (ref: 4.B.2.) of foxgloves and bird which has a faint sketch of a fireplace (thought to be at Melford Hall) on the back. (LLT: 13.A.4)

16 WELSH DRESSER

Sepia pen and ink, inscribed "Gwaynynog. Feb. 1903" and "a Welsh dresser–date 1696". Signed "H.B. Potter", 266 x 230mm.

Extremely finely drawn interior of a corner of a room at Gwaynynog, an old house in Denbigh, North Wales, owned by her uncle, Frederick Burton.

Beatrix Potter described the house in an unfinished story about two bats *(Flittermouse and Fluttermouse)*; she wrote an incomplete story here *(Llewellyn's Well)* in 1911/12, and the garden was used for backgrounds to some of the illustrations in *Flopsy Bunnies*. (LLT: 2.A.3.)

17 TURRET STAIRS

Sepia wash with pencil, inscribed on back "1882", 255 x 160mm.

A very impressive brushwork picture of a spiral staircase, full of perspective, in a tower believed to be St. Mary's church at Birnam, Perthshire.

This staircase was used as a background setting for a painting by Sir John Everett Millais (a close friend of Beatrix Potter's father) titled "The Grey Lady". (BP 287)

18 BEDWELL LODGE

Grey brushwork, inscribed "H.B.P. Oct. 1st–91", 254 x 162 mm.

Shows the main staircase of Bedwell Lodge, near Hatfield, where the Potters spent the summer of 1891. (LLT: 2.A.2)

19 INTERIOR OF GWAYNYNOG

Watercolour, inscribed "March 11–25. 04. Gwaynynog, H.B. Potter"

Interior of the home of Beatrix Potter's uncle, Frederick Burton. (LLT: 12.A.3)

20 INTERIOR OF A BARN

Grey brushwork, inscribed "H.B.P. Oct. 91", 255 x 162mm.

The interior of a barn at Bedwell Lodge, Hertfordshire. (LLT: 12.B.4)

21 PASSAGE WAY

Watercolour, 132 x 180mm.

Drawing, showing an acutely developed sense of perspective, of a passage way on the upper floor of Lennel, Coldstream, Berwickshire. The Potters spent the summer of 1894 at Lennel, a house of which Beatrix Potter wrote (July 17th 1894) as being "large, rambling, roundabout and not overclean". (LLT: 12.A.5.)

22 STAIRWAY AT LINGHOLM

Watercolour, inscribed "Lingholm", 160 x 220mm.

Beatrix Potter spent no less than nine summers between 1885 and 1907 at Lingholm, a large house on the banks of Derwentwater, almost opposite St. Herbert's Island ("Owl Island" of *Squirrel Nutkin*). The house and its extensive grounds play an important role in her writings. It was from here that she outlined the *Squirrel Nutkin* story in a letter to Noel Moore, and the grounds (which are opened to the public during the summer months) feature in many of the backgrounds to the book-illustrations in this book. *Mrs Tiggy-Winkle* also contains backgrounds of Lingholm's grounds (sketched in 1904) and *Tom Kitten* was worked on here (1906). (LLT: 12.A.4)

CASE 4 & 5. HOUSES AND VILLAGE SCENES, AND LANDSCAPES

The pencil, crayon and watercolour drawings in these two sections show a wide variety of subjects, as well as many different styles of drawing. The straight-forwardness of the outline drawing of Bush Hall could be the work of a totally different artist from the one who drew the sepia pen and ink of Lyme Regis.

Likewise the pen and ink of the Swing Gate at Newlands is in a totally different style from the watercolour of Esthwaite Water.

23 LYME REGIS, DORSET

Sepia pen and ink, inscribed "Lyme Regis, H.B. Potter", 268 x 208mm.

Shows a view of the main street leading down to the sea. In 1904, the Potters spent a fortnight at Burley, Lyme Regis, and it was whilst staying here that some of the streets and thatched cottages were drawn and subsequently used as backgrounds for *Little Pig Robinson*. This drawing appears as a background for page 77 of the American large-format edition (1930) of this book. Some of the misplaced drawings for *Benjamin Bunny* were redrawn here. (LLT: 3.B.2.)

24 FARM HOUSE AT BROOKE THORPE
Pen and ink, 267 x 215mm.
Extremely neat and clear pen and ink drawing of a farm house in
Gloucestershire, drawn in October 1904. Beatrix Potter had a block
made from this drawing, possibly for use as a greetings card.
(LLT: 13.A.6)

25 BUSH HALL, HERTFORDSHIRE
Crayon drawing, inscribed "August 15th. 1884", 328 x 223mm.
One of a series of crayon drawings of Bush Hall completed by
Beatrix Potter during the family's stay there from August 1st to
October 3rd 1884. At a later date she has added the following note on
this particular drawing: "These chalk drawings, in singular good per-
spective, must have been done when I was 18. We had a house on the
Lee near Hatfield for 3 months that summer". Beatrix Potter also
wrote in her Journal that Bush Hall—which belonged to Lord
Salisbury—was "an extraordinary scrambling old place, red brick, two
or three stories, tiled, ivied, with little attic windows, low rooms and
long passages". (LLT: 2.B.1.)

26 MELFORD HALL
Watercolour, 227 x 189mm.
Represents one of the side entrances of Melford Hall, the Suffolk home
of Sir William Hyde-Parker, which Beatrix Potter visited on a number
of occasions. (LLT: 13.A.3.)

27 KIRKCUDBRIGHT
Watercolour, inscribed "Kirkcudbright", 140 x 160mm.
Village scene, assumed to have been drawn in the summer of 1899.
(LLT: 14.A.4)

28 SIDMOUTH
Watercolour, inscribed "H.B. Potter, Sidmouth, March 99", 115 x 202mm.
Beatrix Potter visited Sidmouth in Devon a number of times besides
the visit in 1899 when this picture was executed. Parts of *Little Pig
Robinson* were written here and some of the backgrounds for the
illustrations in this book were drawn here. The *Tale* is set in
"Stymouth" (see page 20 of present edition) which is, in fact,
Sidmouth. (LLT: 13.B.3)

29 OLD MARKET HOUSE, AMERSHAM
*Watercolour, inscribed "Amersham Old Market House Aug. 3 1905.
H.B. Potter", 190 x 227mm.*
One of a series of watercolours painted of the picturesque Bucking-
hamshire market town in 1905. Leslie Linder wrote (in *The Art of
Beatrix Potter*, revised edition, 1972): "The Market House was built by

Sir William Drake in 1682. One of the lower arcades was enclosed to make a lock-out. Above the Market House is the room which was the meeting place of the town. Inside the turret is a bell which also dates back to 1682". (LLT: 13.B.2)

30 HILL TOP PORCH IN SNOW
Watercolour, 177 x 148mm.
The slate porch of Hill Top, Beatrix Potter's Lake District home until her marriage to William Heelis, purchased in 1905 with royalties from her books, a small legacy and the sale of some railway bonds. The delightful cottage and farm in Near Sawrey was the setting for many of the books. It was bequeathed to the National Trust in her will. (LLT: 15.A.2)

31 MILL ON THE STOUR
Watercolour, inscribed "An old mill on the Stour, Suffolk. H.B. Potter", 227 x 189mm. (LLT: 13.A.1.)

32 ESTHWAITE WATER AS SEEN FROM LAKEFIELD
Watercolour, inscribed "To illustrate 'line' in landscape. H.B. Potter", 254 x 355mm.
The Potters stayed at Lakefield, a large country house looking out over Esthwaite Water for the first time in the summer of 1896. It was whilst staying at this house on the outskirts of Near Sawrey that Beatrix Potter came to know the village and Hill Top. The house was renamed (*circa* 1902) "Ees Wyke". In 1892, Beatrix Potter wrote: "I have often been laughed at for thinking Esthwaite Water the most beautiful of the lakes". This peaceful stretch of water was the setting for some of the backgrounds to illustrations in *Jeremy Fisher*. (LLT: 3.A.3.)

33 SWING GATE
Sepia pen and ink drawing, 240 x 200mm.
This delightful pen and ink was drawn in September 1904 at Newlands, to the west of Derwentwater. In 1901, whilst staying at Lingholm, near Keswick, the Potter family became friendly with the Reverend Carr, the vicar of Newlands. Beatrix Potter once wrote a set of verses (*The Wanderings of a Small Black Cat*) about an incident which happened to the vicar, and dedicated *Mrs Tiggy-Winkle* to Lucie, one of his two daughters. (LLT: 14.B.5.)

34 VILLAGE ROOF TOPS
Watercolour and pencil, inscribed "March 7.09", 235 x 180mm.
A view over the rooftops of Sawrey, with a note written on the back in the hand of the late Captain K.W.G. Duke RN: "Sawrey from the Tower Bank Arms". The Tower Bank Arms public house, is situated

behind Hill Top and faces the village of Near Sawrey. The inn, with its clock above the doorway, features in one of the illustrations to *Jemima Puddle-Duck.* (BP 1157)

35 FIELD LANDSCAPE IN SNOW
Wash and pencil, inscribed "March 4.09", 250 x 180mm.
This scene, with fields and a line of trees in snow, is thought to be of Sawrey and is the antithesis of her usual style in that bold brush-strokes replace the more customary finely detailed work. (BP 1156)

36 HILL TOP, SAWREY
Sepia pen and ink, 185 x 266mm.
An unfinished look at Hill Top, presumably drawn before or soon after she purchased it as it shows the cottage before the extra wing was added in 1905. (LLT: 15.A.1.)

CASE 6 & 7. GARDEN AND PLANT STUDIES

Beatrix Potter once very modestly wrote that she couldn't invent, only copy, and it is an interesting fact that a large proportion of her book illustrations are set in recognizable surroundings.

For instance, *Squirrel Nutkin* is set in the grounds and surrounding countryside of Lingholm, and *Benjamin Bunny* set in the gardens of Fawe Park, both houses in which the Potter family stayed in the Lake District.

Often these were sketched in the locality and brought back to London to be completed.

As well as views of the gardens, Beatrix Potter also made a large number of still life drawings using leaves and flowers picked in these gardens, echoing a statement made in her *Journal* in 1884 "It is all the same, drawing, painting, modelling, the irresistible desire to copy any beautiful object which strikes the eye."

37 GARDEN PORCH
Watercolour and pencil, 290 x 213mm.
An unfinished watercolour of a door set in a rectangular porch, with bushes and climbing plants either side. (LLT: 4.A.3.)

38 OAK LEAVES
Watercolour, 280 x 390mm.
Two oak twigs with acorns. Note the number of colours used to give a more faithful representation of the actual colour of oak leaves. (LLT: 5.A.1)

39 BEECH TREES
Grey brushwork, inscribed "May 01—Summer is coming, study of Beech tree, unfinished. H.B. Potter". 355 x 255mm. (LLT: 4.A.4.)

40 ELDER BERRIES
Watercolour, 287 x 223mm. (LLT: 5.A.4.)

41 WILD YELLOW BALSAM
Watercolour, inscribed "Wild Yellow Balsam. Derwentwater Cumberland, also Coniston. Impatiens Noli-me-tangere. Beatrix Potter". 278 x 215mm.
The note on this drawing, and on the watercolour of Sea Lavender on display in this case, demonstrates the meticulous care with which Beatrix Potter noted place found, common and Latin name of each specimen etc. on her natural history drawings, showing that they were drawn as scientific examples rather than as an artist's exercise. (LLT: 15.B.6)

42 SNOWDROPS
Watercolour, 163 x 131mm. (LLT: 15.B.2)

43 FLOWER STUDY
Watercolour, 135 x 133mm. (LLT: 15.B.1.)

44 SEA LAVENDER
Watercolour, inscribed "Sea Lavendar. Statice Limonium. Kirkcudbright Bay. Sept. 99", 290 x 240mm.(LLT: 15.B.5)

45 AN ENGLISH GARDEN, LAKEFIELD
Pen, ink and watercolour, inscribed "Aug. An English Garden—Lakefield", 300 x 290mm.
Painting of a walled garden at Lakefield, Sawrey, with Coniston Fells in the background. In her late twenties, Beatrix Potter joined a small drawing circle who circulated a portfolio of members' pictures for criticism, each member signing his criticism and work with a pen-name. Beatrix Potter's pseudonym, rather predictably perhaps, was "Bunny", and this name appears on the back of this garden scene. There is also a partly torn-off comment: "wanting in colour and life in distance". (BP 238)

46 WILDFLOWERS
Watercolour, 317 x 232mm.
A group of wildflowers in an out-door setting, on the back of which is an unfinished painting of wild vetch. Flowers include honeysuckle, saw-wort, cow parsley, buttercup, forget-me-not, cornflower, and scabious. (LLT: 4.B.1)

47 AUTUMN BERRIES
Watercolour, inscribed "Autumn Berries. H.B. Potter", 276 x 386mm.
Two twigs, the top one (hawthorn) bearing bright red berries.
(LLT: 5.A.2.)

48 LAKEFIELD, SAWREY
Watercolour, inscribed "At Evening's close—H.B. Potter—Ees Wyke, then Lakefield", 292 x 227mm.
Lakefield (renamed Ees Wyke *circa* 1902) is a country house in Near Sawrey which the Potters rented in 1896. This watercolour, one of many of the gardens of Lakefield, shows a wooden gate under a foliage arch, with Coniston Fells in the distance. (LLT: 4.A.2.)

49 MARGUERITES
Watercolour, 138 x 130mm. (LLT: 15.B.3.)

50 A GARDEN SCENE, GWAYNYNOG
Sepia pen and ink, inscribed "Gwaynynog, Nov. 5th. 04", 266 x 210mm.
Gwaynynog, a Denbighshire house bearing the date 1571, was the ancestral home of the Myddletons, had associations with Dr. Johnson, and belonged to Beatrix Potter's uncle, Frederick Burton. The garden was used as a setting for certain illustrations to *Flopsy Bunnies.* She wrote of the garden in 1895: "very large, two-thirds surrounded by a red brick wall with many apricots, and an inner circle of old grey apple trees on wooden espaliers. It is very productive but not tidy, the prettiest kind of garden, where bright old fashioned flowers grow amongst the currant bushes". (LLT: 27.A.4)

51 AUTUMN LEAVES
Watercolour, inscribed "Autumn", 142 x 253mm. (LLT: 10.B.1)

52 LEAVES OF A SWEET BAY TREE
Watercolour, inscribed on back "H.B. Potter, S.B., 1900", 180 x 255mm.
Two twigs of bay leaves. Top left, with arrow above the top twig, is written: "direct light from this side". Bottom right, with another arrow, is the note: "against the light. The veins in the leaf are slightly transparent. There has been no sunshine & evergreen leaves show very little transparent light without it". (BP. 269)

CASE 8 & 9.   NATURAL HISTORY AND MICROSCOPIC WORK

   Perhaps the least known facet of Beatrix Potter can be seen in this section—Beatrix Potter the scientist.
   Beatrix Potter was a keen naturalist, not just on the fanciful level of

the book illustrations but also on a more scientific level. It is perhaps because of this that the animals in the book illustrations keep their animal characteristics even whilst dressed in human clothing.

She spent many hours studying and drawing in the galleries of the Natural History Museum near her home in South Kensington, and she had her own microscope under which she could study insects she had collected.

As with so much of her work, it is the fine detail and meticulous care which are the most striking aspects of the studies in this section.

53 MICROSCOPIC STUDIES OF A BEETLE
Watercolour, pen and ink, 268 x 365mm.
Line drawing of a beetle, with highly magnified study of part of its anatomy. (LLT: 6.B.3)

54 HIGHLY MAGNIFIED WATER FLEA (?)
Watercolour, inscribed "April 1st. 87. from Camfield—Castor", 270 x 366mm.
A study, thought to be of water Daphnaea. The inscription is confusing. Camfield Place is a country house in Hertfordshire which belonged to Beatrix Potter's grandparents. Castor was thought to be the name of the subject of the study, but various authorities contacted state they know of no such creature. However, there is a small village near Peterborough, Northants, called Castor, so one must assume that this creature, very much like a species of water flea, was discovered at Castor on a visit from Camfield, where Beatrix Potter often stayed. (LLT: 7.B.2.)

55 TWO SKULLS
Sepia drawings, 140 x 135mm.
Believed to have been drawn in 1887 (?). (LLT: 17.A.3)

56 STUDIES OF BEES, ETC.
Watercolour, 112 x 176mm. (LLT: 19.B.5)

57 "TICK"
Watercolour, 240 x 304mm.
Study of a tick, highly magnified. Leslie Linder writes: "A tick is the common name for several kinds of mites or acarids which infest the hair or fur of various animals, e.g. sheep-tick". (LLT: 7.B.1)

58 DRAWING OF A SKULL
Pen and ink drawing, 130 x 150mm. (LLT: 17.A.4)

59 PRIVET HAWK-MOTH, ETC.
Watercolour, inscribed "Feb. 87", 244 x 268mm.
The privet hawk-moth, caterpillar and chrysalis, drawn actual size, with a highly magnified watercolour of the wing scales. (LLT: 6.B.1)

60 MICROSCOPIC STUDY OF A SPIDER
Watercolour, inscribed "July 11th. 87. Lingholm, Keswick", 270 x 366mm.
(LLT: 7.A.3)

61 MICROSCOPIC STUDY OF A SPIDER
Watercolour, inscribed "Lingholm", 268 x 362mm.
A male crab-spider *Xysticus cristatus* (Clerck), magnified x 30. A study made *circa* 1887. (LLT: 7.A.1.)

62 FEET OF A LOBSTER
Watercolour, inscribed "March 85", 268 x 260mm. (LLT: 7.B.3)

63 LITHOGRAPH OF PRIVET HAWK-MOTH ETC.
280 x 380mm. (LLT: 17.A.1.)

64 LITHOGRAPH OF MISCELLANEOUS SUBJECTS
222 x 286mm. (LLT: 17.A.2)
Circa 1896, Beatrix Potter prepared twelve plates for a Miss Martineau of the Natural History Museum, South Kensington, all of scientific nature. Only the two lithographs exhibited appear to have been completed, printed by West Newman of Hatton Garden.

65 SKETCHES OF NEWTS
a) inscribed "May 86", 75 x 115mm, illustrates the male.
b) 90 x 180mm, shows the male in breeding season (about April).
c) inscribed "May 86", 75 x 114mm, shows the female.
Three watercolours in one mount, all brightly coloured. (LLT: 19.B.1)

66 LIZARDS
Watercolour, inscribed "1885", 135 x 184mm. (LLT: 19.B.2)

CASE 10. FUNGI

Some years before the birth of the *Tale of Peter Rabbit* Beatrix Potter was planning a book of a totally different nature. Between 1893 and 1898 she had made an extensive study of British fungi, collecting, studying and drawing specimens found on holidays in the Lake District or Scotland.

Such was her interest that a paper she had written on the germination of the spores of *Agaricineae* was read at a meeting of an important natural history society, the Linnean Society, on April 1st 1897.

Her proposed book on fungi was never completed, but forty-nine of her drawings were later used to illustrate W.P.K. Findlay's *Wayside and Woodland Fungi* (F. Warne, 1967).

67 BOLETUS SCABER
Watercolour, inscribed "Lingholm, Keswick, Oct. 97", 298 x 423mm.
Three fungi inscribed with the place they were found: "Silver Hill. Oct. 10th"; "Boat Oct. 6th" and "Corner. Oct. 8th", and a section. Boletus Scaber (commonly called the "Brown Birch Boletus") is common in the woods of Lingholm. This fungus features in a short story (*A Walk Amongst the Fungi*) which Beatrix Potter intended to form part of a never-completed sequel to *The Fairy Caravan*. (LLT: 6.A.2)

68 PEZIZA AURENTIA
Watercolour, inscribed "HBP" on front and "Beatrix Potter Oct. 1893" on back, 215 x 280mm.
Study of the beautiful orange coloured fungus *Peziza aurentia* or "Orange Peel Fungus", shown amongst fallen leaves. On the back is a note (not in Beatrix Potter's handwriting) concluding: ". . . the specimens painted by Miss Potter were found in the woods of Strathallan by the Hon. Frances Drummond–Oct. 1893". (BP. 354)

69 YELLOW GRISETTE AND SCARLET FLY CAP
Watercolour, pen and ink, 310 x 430mm.
Four fungi and a section. Left side are two examples of Yellow Grisette, one of the Amanitopsis group of fungi, inscribed "Ullock, Sept. 2nd. 97". Right side shows "Scarlet Fly Cap" (also known as the "Fly Agaric") *Amanita muscaria*, with a section. Inscribed "Sept. 3. 97". (BP. 244)

70 COPRINUS AND DEATH CAP
Watercolour, 298 x 423mm.
Fungi, with pencil outline of spores and a vertical section. On the left is drawn *Coprinus* (often known as "inky caps" because of the black ink resulting from the caps liquefying as the spores ripen), with an outline pencil sketch of the spores. Inscribed below: "Sept. 24th 97. Lingholm, Keswick" and "Coprinus" on back. On the right is *Amanita phalloides*, the deadly poisonous "Death Cap" with inscription below section: "Sept. 25th. 97, Lingholm, Keswick" and on back "Death Cap. Amanita phalloides". (LLT: 6.A.1)

71 PAINTING OF A FUNGUS
Watercolour, inscribed "Lingholm, Aug. 14th. 88", 272 x 213mm.
Name of fungus unknown. (LLT: 16.B.4)

72 LACTARIUS
Watercolour, inscribed "?Lactarius", 190 x 252mm. (LLT: 16.B.3)

73 LACTARIUS
Watercolour, inscribed as above, 182 x 257mm. (LLT: 16.B.2)
Lactarius, or "Milky Caps", is a large genus of agarics with very brittle flesh, not poisonous but unpleasant to the taste. Named after the presence of latex, which appears when the cap is broken.

74 HYGROPHORUS
Watercolour, inscribed "Lingholm, Sept. 3rd. 88. Hygrophorus '? puniceus' ", 212 x 280mm.
Hygrophorous puniceus is commonly known as the "Crimson Wax Cap", named from the blood red (*puniceus* is Latin for this colour) caps which make it stand out in fields and meadows in late August onwards. (LLT: 16.B.1)

CASE 11 & 12.   ANIMAL STUDIES

The drawings in this section range from pencil sketches where animal characteristics are captured in a few quick lines, to completed watercolours.
They were drawn from her pets or from the animals on her Lake District farm.

75 HORSES AND COWS
Pencil sketch, 250 x 175mm. (LLT: 17.B.5)

76 SHEEP AND COWS
Pen and ink sketches, 250 x 175mm. (LLT: 17.B.3.)

77 RAM'S HEAD
Grey brushwork, inscribed "Ram's Head, drawn from a stuffed specimen, Beatrix Potter", 284 x 354mm. (LLT: 5.B.3)

78 HEAD OF A ROE DEER
Grey brushwork, inscribed "Roe-deer's head, drawn from a stuffed specimen, natural size, Beatrix Potter", 368 x 290mm.
Although drawn from a stuffed head, probably from a specimen in the Natural History Museum, Beatrix Potter has brought this animal to life and everything about it is very real. There used to be an adage that the eyes in a good portrait painting tend to follow you around the room, and this is certainly true of the eyes in this work which have all the softness and life of a live deer. (LLT: 5.B.1)

79 FARMYARD SKETCHES
    Pencil sketches, 176 x 250mm.
    Sketches of horses, sheep and cows. (LLT: 17.B.6)

80 STUDIES OF A DEAD THRUSH
    Pen, ink and watercolour, inscribed "Woodcote 1902 picked up dead in the snow", 225 x 290mm.
    Nine drawings of a thrush from various angles. On the back is the inscription "Studies of a dead thrush". Also on the back is a sketch of rabbits, with note. "Rabbits from life. H.B. Potter". (BP. 418)

81 GUINEA-PIGS IN A BASKET
    Watercolour, 226 x 150mm.
    Three guinea-pigs in a wicker basket with raised lid. In her Journal for February 5th 1893, Beatrix Potter tells of how she borrowed some guinea-pigs from a London neighbour, Miss Paget, one of which died whilst in her care. These are almost certainly those drawn in this picture. In the Leslie Linder Trust Collection (housed in National Book League) there is another watercolour (ref: 18.A.5) of the underside of the basket used for this picture. (LLT: 18.A.1.)

82 WOOD MOUSE
    Watercolour, inscribed "Wood Mouse, Christmas 1886, Beatrix Potter", 75 x 110mm.
    Leslie Linder wrote: "This little mouse has magnificent whiskers and a long, curly tail. The picture was sent as a Christmas present to one of Beatrix Potter's friends". (LLT: 18.A.2)

83 STUDIES OF RABBITS
    Pencil drawing, 255 x 162mm. (LLT: 18.B.5.)

84 WEASEL
    Watercolour, inscribed "Camfield, May 88". 193 x 280mm.
    This drawing was made at Camfield Place, the Hertfordshire home of her uncle, Frederick Burton, and his wife, Harriet. Of her aunt, Beatrix Potter wrote in her *Journal*: "How amusing Aunt Harriet is, she is more like a weasel than ever". (LLT: 19.A.5)

85 STUDIES OF CATS
    Pencil drawing, 253 x 160mm.
    Studies in pencil of sleeping cats and of the faces of cats. Leslie Linder suggests these were probably studies made for the *Tom Kitten* story. (LLT: 19.A.1)

86   STUDIES OF BATS
  a) 90 x 110mm, inscribed "Oct. 88"
  b) 115 x 90mm.
  c) 90 x 113mm, inscribed "September 10th. 87. Lingholm"
  Three watercolours in one mount. (LLT: 19.B.3)

87   WATER TORTOISE OR TERRAPIN
  Watercolour, 100 x 155mm.
  In the Leslie Linder Trust Collection (housed in the Mark Longman
  Library at the National Book League) there is a pen and ink drawing
  (LLT: 12.A.1.) of the schoolroom of 2, Bolton Gardens. In the fore-
  ground is a small tortoise, presumably the same as that in this
  exhibited watercolour. (LLT: 19.A.4)

88   STUDIES OF MICE
  Pencil, inscribed "Thurs. 2.", 200 x 165mm.
  Sketches of mice from almost every angle. (BP. 388)

89   SKETCHES OF HEDGEHOGS
  Sepia pen and ink and watercolour, 160 x 160mm.
  Studies for illustrations to *The Tale of Mrs Tiggy-Winkle.* (LLT: 25.B.4)

90   HEADS OF RATS
  Watercolour, 175 x 200mm.
  Beatrix Potter had no problems in obtaining models for her drawings
  of rats, for they so over ran Hill Top that Mrs Cannon, the wife of the
  farmer who managed the farm for her, had four or five cats. It was
  because of the rats that zinc was put on the bottom of the doors in
  Hill Top and the skirtings were done in concrete. However, the rats
  also proved useful for evidently they provided the inspiration for
  The Roly-Poly Pudding. (LLT: 19.A.2)

91   STUDIES OF A BAT
  Watercolour, inscribed "Jan. 24. 85"
  Two views of a bat, beautifully drawn and coloured. Painted when she
  was eighteen, probably from a specimen at the Natural History
  Museum, South Kensington. (LLT: 19.B.4)